B♭ Book

Selections from

STAR WARS®

Music by JOHN WILLIAMS

Arranged for Solos, Duets and Trios by Tony Esposito

Background instruments performed and arranged by Andy Selby

Published in the following editions:
C Book, B♭ Book, E♭ Book, Bass Clef Book and Piano Accompaniment.
All books are compatible with each other and are playable in any combination.

Project Manager: TONY ESPOSITO
Art Layout: JOE KLUCAR

BREAKDOWN OF PARTS

The twelve arrangements in *Selections from Star Wars* can sucessfully be played as solo, duets or trios, with or without the piano accompaniment. Any combination of these parts—C, B♭, E♭, Bass Clef and Piano Accompaniment—may be used, although some mixes will be better than others.

The following instruments can and are encouraged to participate:

C BOOK	Piccolo, Flute, Oboe, Violin, Guitar
B♭ BOOK	Trumpet, Clarinet, Tenor Sax, Soprano Sax, Bass Clarinet, Baritone T.C.
E♭ BOOK	Alto Sax, Baritone Sax
BASS CLEF BOOK	Trombone, Baritone B.C., Bassoon, Cello
PIANO ACCOMP.	Organ, Synthesizer

FIRST LINE	SOLO PART
SECOND LINE	DUET PART
THIRD LINE	TRIO PART

In order to enhance musicality and create interest, a considerable amount of contrapuntal writing is included in these arrangements. Although the parts are not technically difficult, rhythmic confidence and part independence will be required for satisfactory results.

HOW TO PLAY WITH THE PLAY-ALONG CD

The CD was produced to provide you, the player, with an audio educational tool that will enable you to perform in an orchestral setting.

For those of you who will play the first (lead) part, you will have to play the melody using the same phrasing as the orchestral instruments that may be doubling your part. To be able to do this efficiently, I suggest playing your part alone until you are familiar with the melody as it is written before attempting to play along with the CD.

Only when you have mastered the melodic line can you follow the orchestral phrasing, and in time you will develop your own style.

For those of you who will be playing the second and third parts, your job is to LISTEN! You must listen to your own part first, listen to the third harmony (or second if you are playing the third part) and then blend with the lead, who will usually be playing the melody. When playing with the CD, you should concentrate on what is written and not what you hear; it will all come together soon.

For some of the young players who have not yet had the experience of playing with a band, this project will surely open your mind and ears and will prepare you to play someday with your dream band.

TRACKING

CONTENTS

CANTINA BAND

By **JOHN WILLIAMS**
Arranged by TONY ESPOSITO

Moderate rag feel ♩ = 230

Cantina Band - 5 - 1
IF9917CD

10

Cantina Band - 5 - 4

Rag feel

THE IMPERIAL MARCH
(Darth Vader's Theme)

By **JOHN WILLIAMS**
Arranged by TONY ESPOSITO

The Imperial March - 3 - 1
IF9917CD

14

The Imperial March - 3 - 2
IF9917CD

HAN SOLO AND THE PRINCESS

By **JOHN WILLIAMS**
Arranged by TONY ESPOSITO

Moderately, with expression

Han Solo and the Princess - 2 - 1
IF9917CD

Han Solo and the Princess - 2 - 2
IF9917CD

MAY THE FORCE BE WITH YOU

By **JOHN WILLIAMS**
Arranged by TONY ESPOSITO

May the Force Be With You - 2 - 1
IF9917CD

May the Force Be With You - 2 - 2
IF9917CD

PARADE OF THE EWOKS

By **JOHN WILLIAMS**
Arranged by TONY ESPOSITO

Parade of the Ewoks - 4 - 1
IF9917CD

Parade of the Ewoks - 4 - 2
IF9917CD

22

Parade of the Ewoks - 4 - 3
IF9917CD

Parade of the Ewoks - 4 - 4
IF9917CD

PRINCESS LEIA'S THEME

By **JOHN WILLIAMS**
Arranged by TONY ESPOSITO

Moderately slow, but moving

Princess Leia's Theme - 3 - 1
IF9917CD

Solo

Tutti

Princess Leia's Theme - 3 - 2
IF9917CD

26

YODA'S THEME

By **JOHN WILLIAMS**
Arranged by TONY ESPOSITO

Yoda's Theme - 3 - 1
IF9917CD

28

THE THRONE ROOM

By **JOHN WILLIAMS**
Arranged by TONY ESPOSITO

The Throne Room - 4 - 1
IF9917CD

ANAKIN'S THEME

By **JOHN WILLIAMS**
Arranged by TONY ESPOSITO

Majestically

Anakin's Theme - 4 - 4
IF9917CD

DUEL OF THE FATES

By **JOHN WILLIAMS**
Arranged by TONY ESPOSITO

Duel of the Fates - 6 - 1
IF9917CD

Duel of the Fates - 6 - 3
IF9917CD

42

Duel of the Fates - 6 - 5
IF9917CD

STAR WARS
(Main Theme)

By **JOHN WILLIAMS**
Arranged by TONY ESPOSITO

Star Wars (Main Theme) - 2 - 1
IF9917CD

Star Wars (Main Theme) - 2 - 2
IF9917CD

VICTORY CELEBRATION

By **JOHN WILLIAMS**
Arranged by TONY ESPOSITO

Victory Celebration - 3 - 1
IF9917CD

Victory Celebration - 3 - 2
IF9917CD

48